THIRD EDITION

grade 4

MUSIC THEORY
for Young Musicians

Study Notes with Exercises for ABRSM Theory Exams

Name : ···

Address : ···

Phone : ···

NEW SYLLABUS

YING YING NG

pocostudio
MAKE SENSE OF MUSIC

Published by:
Poco Studio Sdn Bhd (646228-V)
B-2-8, IOI Boulevard, Jalan Kenari 5, Bandar Puchong Jaya, 47170 Puchong, Selangor, Malaysia
+60 13-618 5289 (WhatsApp)   poco_studio@yahoo.co.uk   facebook.com/pocostudio

Copyediting by David C. L. Ngo BAI, PhD, SMIEEE

Printed in Malaysia

ISBN 978-967-10003-4-2

PREFACE

Designed as a workbook to suit the needs of today's young pupils and their teachers, this series presents music theory in a very easy to understand and practical format. Here are some of the pedagogical principles adopted, which make this series unique:

Problem Solving: Breaking a problem into smaller parts makes solving it easier. This series isolates a problem, breaks it into small, manageable parts, and then merges it back into the bigger picture.

Repetition: The key to learning music theory is repetition. Under the lesson plan, the pupil studies component parts incrementally, applying previously acquired skills in the repetitive drills of subsequent lessons.

Association: Children will not learn if repetition is dull. The series creates a fantasy world by using pictures, cartoons and stories to introduce new key words and concepts; this arouses the interest and invokes the imagination of the child, thereby aiding retention of the information.

Challenge: Examinations can provide a challenge to the pupil. This series covers the latest revisions outlined by the Associated Board of the Royal Schools of Music for their theory examinations. It uses effective and efficient drills and exercises that progressively teach the basic concepts. The material is simplified to suit the child's level. The examples and exercises build on language and concepts that children already have, culminating in the acquisition of the skills and knowledge vital to passing the examination.

NOTES ON THE THIRD EDITION
The 3rd edition of Music Theory for Young Musicians brings the practice exercises and examples in the text up to date with the latest ABRSM exam requirements. Incorporated with exam-oriented terms, instructions given are made simple and clear for each exercise; they serve to familiarize the students with the format and content of the ABRSM exam while making them easy to understand. To support exam preparation, this edition includes revision notes on the key areas and a specimen test in the exam format. Exercises and drills are revised to reflect the changes to the new syllabus and format.

ACKNOWLEDGE
Cover design and assistance with the illustrations by Amos Tai is gratefully acknowledged. I also extend my sincere thanks to the following persons for advice and suggestions as reviewers of the draft:

- Margaret O'Sullivan Farrell BMus, DipMus, LTCL
  Course Director, Lecturer in Keyboard Studies
  DIT Conservatory of Music and Drama, Dublin, Ireland

- Dr. Ita Beausang BMus, MA, PhD, LRAM
  Former Acting Director, Lecturer in Musicianship Studies
  DIT Conservatory of Music and Drama, Dublin, Ireland

Their suggestions for its improvement have helped immeasurably to make it a useful and practical workbook. My grateful thanks also go to my family, David, Alethia and Natasha, for their patience and love that have allowed me to pursue this project.

Ying Ying Ng

CONTENTS

Alto Clef

Alto clef

- In the **alto clef**, middle C is on the middle line. • As the range of the viola is between the treble and bass clef, the viola uses the alto clef, so that its notes can be written with a minimum of ledger lines.

C D E F G A B middle C D E F G A B C

---

1 **Fill in as semibreves** (whole-notes) **the missing notes and their letter names.**

a

ascending C ☐ ☐ ☐ ☐ ☐ ☐ ☐

b

descending C ☐ ☐ ☐ ☐ ☐ ☐ ☐

---

2 **Write the letter names.**

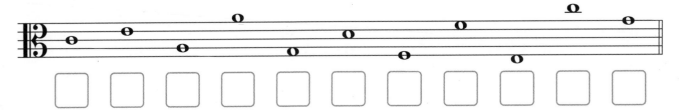

☐ ☐ ☐ ☐ ☐ ☐ ☐ ☐ ☐ ☐ ☐

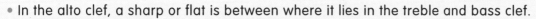

2 • In the alto clef, a sharp or flat is between where it lies in the treble and bass clef.

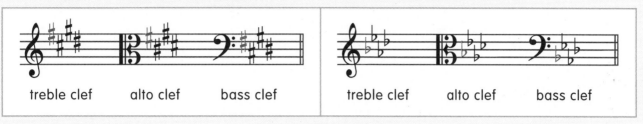

| treble clef | alto clef | bass clef | treble clef | alto clef | bass clef |

3 Write the alto clef and key signature for each key. Name the other key that has the same key signature.

[a] G major   [b] D major   [c] A major   [d] E major

> E minor

[e] F major   [f] B♭ major   [g] E♭ major   [h] A♭ major

4 Write the **tonic triad** of each key, using a key signature.

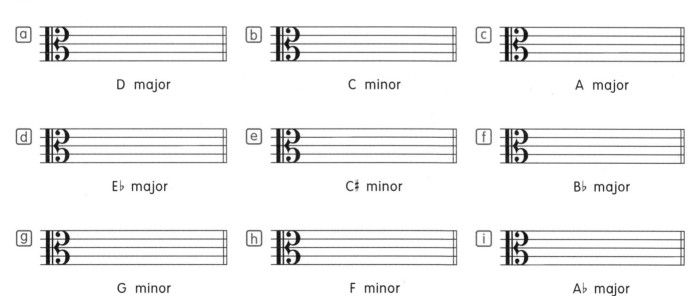

[a] D major   [b] C minor   [c] A major

[d] E♭ major   [e] C♯ minor   [f] B♭ major

[g] G minor   [h] F minor   [i] A♭ major

5 Rewrite the alto notes at the same pitch in the treble and bass clef.

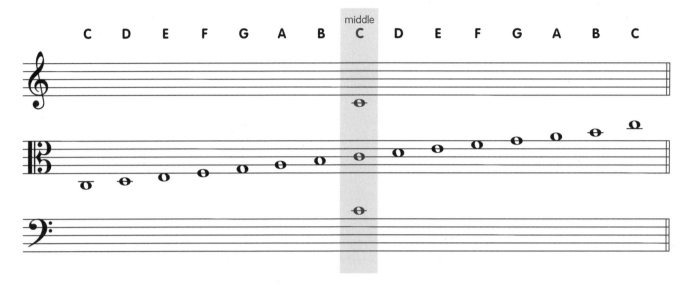

6 Rewrite each note at the same pitch in the alto clef.

7 Rewrite each alto note at the same pitch in the given clef.

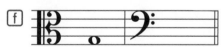

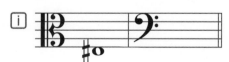

8 Rewrite each melody at the same pitch in the alto clef.

9 Rewrite each melody at the same pitch in the given clef.

Breves, Double Dots and Duplets

Breves

- A **breve** (double whole-note) is worth 2 semibreves (whole-notes).
- A **breve rest** (double whole-note rest) is used for a whole bar's rest in $\frac{4}{2}$.

Time name	Note	Rest
breve (double whole-note)		

1 Rewrite each melody in notes and rests of twice the value. **(Add the new time signature.)**

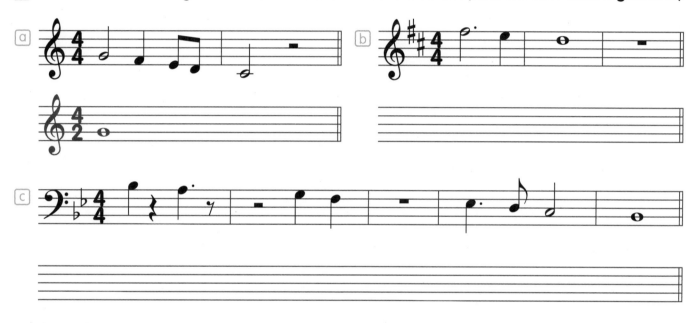

2 Rewrite each melody in notes and rests of half the value. **(Add the new time signature.)**

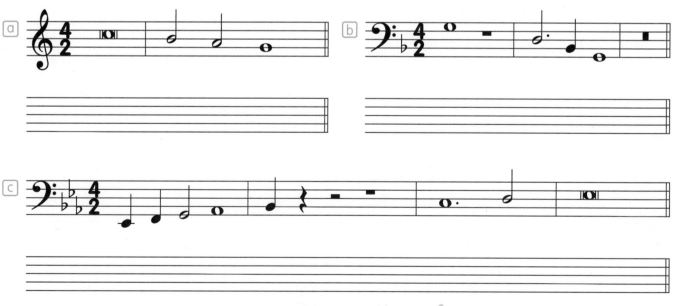

Double dots

- The **1st dot** adds half the value of the note; the **2nd dot** adds half the value of the 1st dot.

double dotted semibreve
(double dotted whole-note)

- A double dotted note is usually followed by a note ¼ the basic note value.

$$\mathbf{o}\cdot\cdot \quad \textstyle\int \;=\; \mathbf{o} \;+\; \textstyle\int \;+\; \textstyle\int \;+\; \textstyle\int \;=\; 2\ \mathbf{o}$$

value   =   1   +   ½   +   ¼   +   ¼   =   2

1

3 Fill in the notes.

a. double dotted minim
(double dotted half-note)

b. double dotted crotchet
(double dotted quarter-note)

c. double dotted quaver
(double dotted eighth-note)

4 Fill in the notes and number.

5 Add one rest at each ∗.

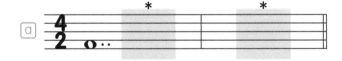

Duplets

- A **duplet** is 2 notes played in the time of 3.

Duplet		In the time of:
	or	
	or	
	or	

6 **Add the time signature.**

a

b

c

d

e

f

7 **Add the missing bar-lines.**

a

b

c

Time Signatures

Time signatures for grade 4

	Simple time	Compound time
Duple	**2/2** ♩ ♩ 2 **minim** beats (half-note)	**6/4** ♩. ♩. 2 **dotted minim** beats (dotted half-note)
	2/4 ♩ ♩ 2 **crotchet** beats (quarter-note)	**6/8** ♩. ♩. 2 **dotted crotchet** beats (dotted quarter-note)
		6/16 ♪. ♪. 2 **dotted quaver** beats (dotted eighth-note)
Triple	**3/2** ♩ ♩ ♩ 3 **minim** beats (half-note)	**9/4** ♩. ♩. ♩. 3 **dotted minim** beats (dotted half-note)
	3/4 ♩ ♩ ♩ 3 **crotchet** beats (quarter-note)	**9/8** ♩. ♩. ♩. 3 **dotted crotchet** beats (dotted quarter-note)
	3/8 ♪ ♪ ♪ 3 **quaver** beats (eighth-note)	**9/16** ♪. ♪. ♪. 3 **dotted quaver** beats (dotted eighth-note)
Quadruple	**4/2** ♩ ♩ ♩ ♩ 4 **minim** beats (half-note)	**12/4** ♩. ♩. ♩. ♩. 4 **dotted minim** beats (dotted half-note)
	4/4 ♩ ♩ ♩ ♩ 4 **crotchet** beats (quarter-note)	**12/8** ♩. ♩. ♩. ♩. 4 **dotted crotchet** beats (dotted quarter-note)
	4/8 ♪ ♪ ♪ ♪ 4 **quaver** beats (eighth-note)	**12/16** ♪. ♪. ♪. ♪. 4 **dotted quaver** beats (dotted eighth-note)

1 Complete the time signature, and describe it (simple/compound; duple/triple/quadruple).

a) 4 ...

compound duple

b) 4 ...

c) 8 ...

d) 16 ...

e) 4 ...

f) 16 ...

g) 6 ...

h) 9 ...

i) 4 ...

j) 6 ...

k) 9 ...

l) 12 ...

Grouping of notes in compound time:

- Group (or beam) notes in:

dotted crotchet beats	dotted minim beats	dotted quaver beats
(dotted quarter-note beats)	(dotted half-note beats)	(dotted eighth-note beats)

 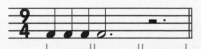 

- Apply the same rules for grouping notes in **6 9 12** in **6 9 12 6 9 12** , except that the time
  8 8 8 **4 4 4 16 16 16**

  values are: **doubled** in **6 9 12** , and **halved** in **6 9 12** .
  4 4 4 **16 16 16**

 Grouping of notes in **6 9 12** : pp. 23-25 in Music Theory for Young Musicians Grade 3, 3rd Ed.
8 8 8

2 **Add the missing bar-lines.**

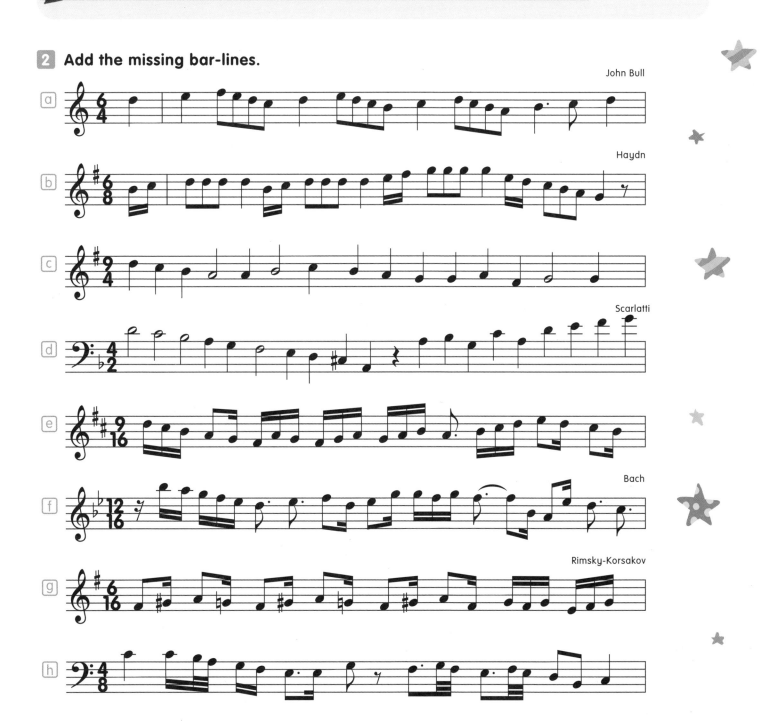

Changing the time signature

Twice and half the value

❶ Keep the same number of beats (or top number).
❷ Change the type of beat (or bottom number):

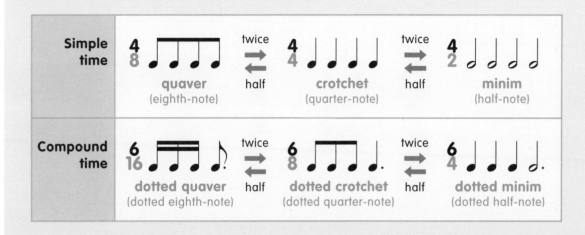

3 Rewrite each rhythm in notes and rests of twice the value. (Add the new time signature.)

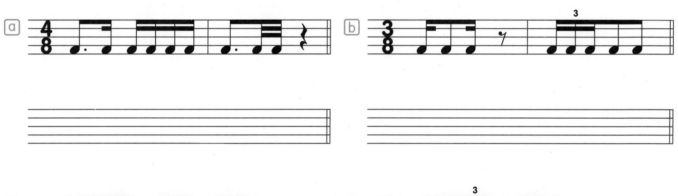

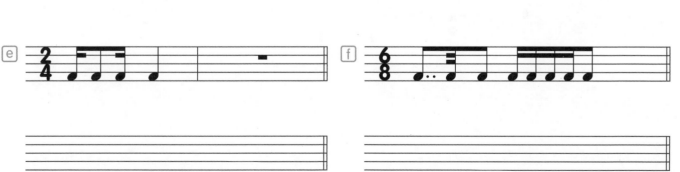

4 Rewrite each rhythm in notes and rests of half the value. (Add the new time signature.)

2 Simple to compound

❶ Multiply the top number by 3 and the bottom number by 2.
❷ Change undotted beats to dotted beats.
❸ Change triplets to normal ('3' removed).
❹ Change beats divided into 2 to duplets ('2' added).

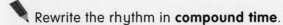

Rewrite the rhythm in **compound time**.

Simple time	
Compound time	

5 **Rewrite each rhythm in** compound time. **(Add the new time signature.)**

ⓐ

ⓑ

ⓒ

ⓓ

ⓔ

ⓕ

Compound to simple

❶ Divide the top number by 3 and the bottom number by 2.
❷ Change dotted beats to undotted beats.
❸ Change beats divided into 3 to triplets ('3' added).
❹ Change duplets to normal ('2' removed).

Rewrite the rhythm in **simple time**.

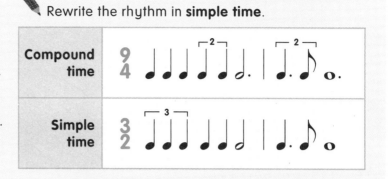

6 Rewrite each rhythm in simple time. (Add the new time signature.)

7 Rewrite each melody with the notes correctly grouped (or beamed).

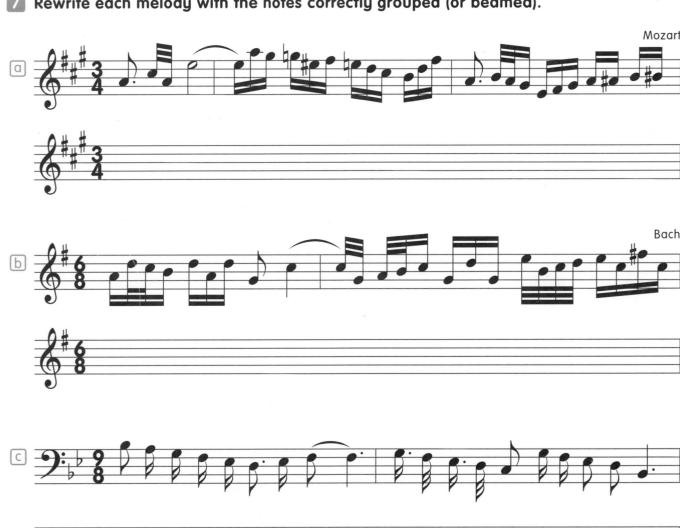

Finding deliberate mistakes

- In grade 4, you might be asked to find 5 deliberate mistakes in a piece of music.

Kinds of mistake: pp. 28-29 in Music Theory for Young Musicians Grade 3, 3rd Ed.

8 **Circle 5 deliberate mistakes in each melody, and rewrite it correctly.**

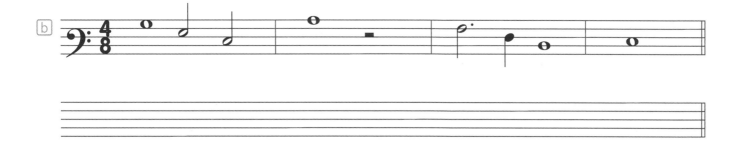

Four-Bar Rhythms

Composing a 4-bar rhythm

- **Time signature**. Look at the time signature and see how many/what type of beats there will be in each bar. • **Plan**. Use a plan like A-A1-A2-B. • **Rhythmic pattern**. Keep patterns from the opening.
- **Upbeat**. Make sure the upbeat and last bar add up to 1 whole bar, and the 2nd phrase starts at the end of the 1st bar. • **Ending**. Finish on a long note.

Compose a 4-bar rhythm using A-A1-A2-B.

- Phrase 1 **A** : Given pattern
- Phrase 3 **A2** : Another variation of A
- Phrase 2 **A1** : Variation of A
- Phrase 4 **B** : New pattern

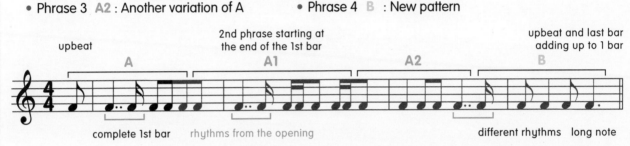

---

1 Write a 4-bar rhythm using the opening.

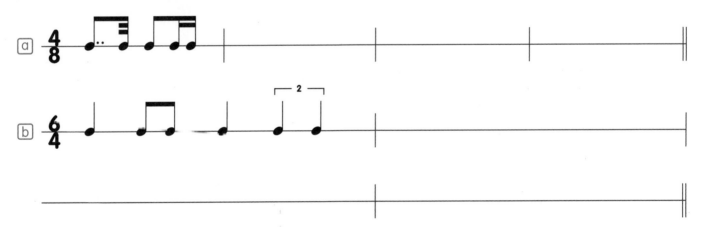

---

2 Write a 4-bar rhythm using the opening, which begins on an upbeat.

3 Write a 4-bar rhythm using the opening. (Complete the 1st bar.)

a) $\frac{3}{4}$

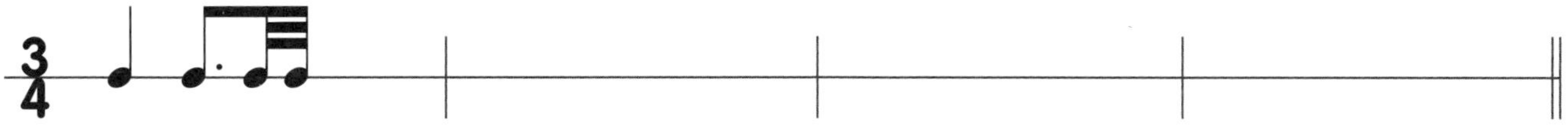

b) $\frac{6}{16}$

c) $\frac{4}{2}$

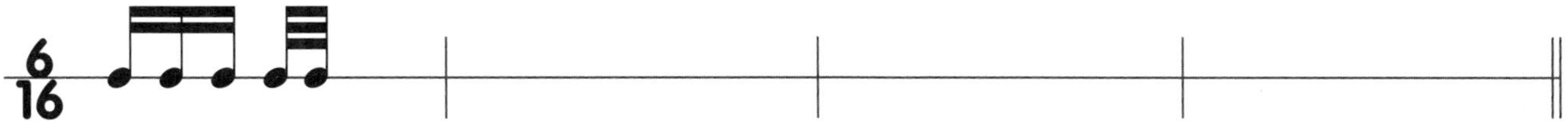

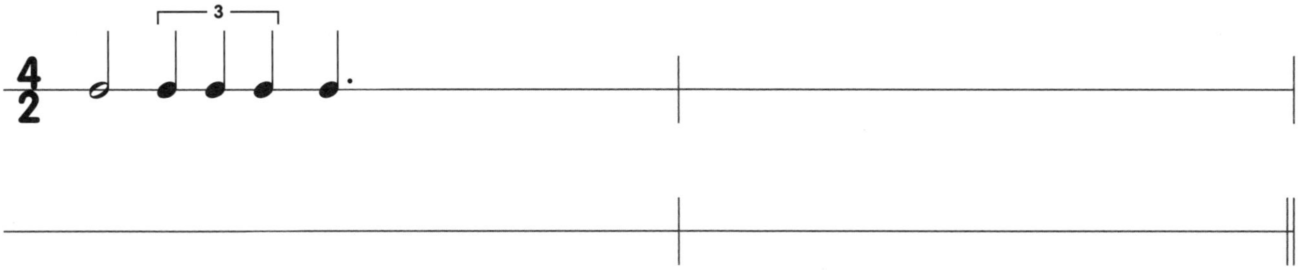

4 Write a 4-bar rhythm using the opening, which begins on an upbeat. (Complete the 1st bar.)

a) $\frac{6}{8}$

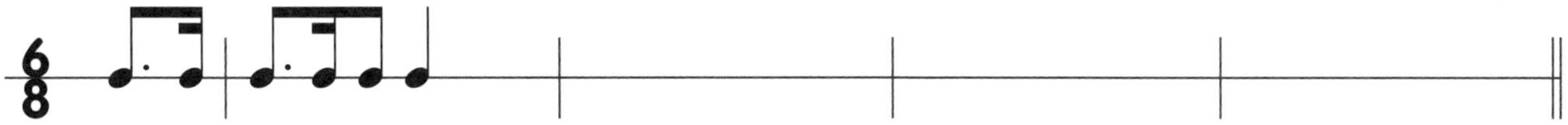

b) $\frac{3}{2}$

c) $\frac{4}{4}$

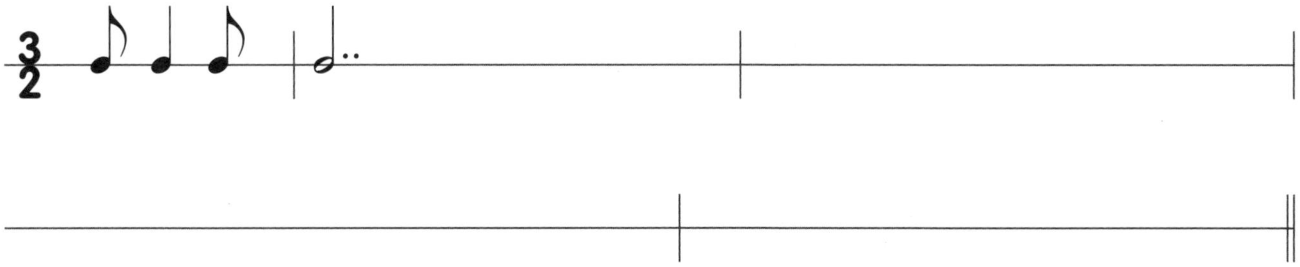

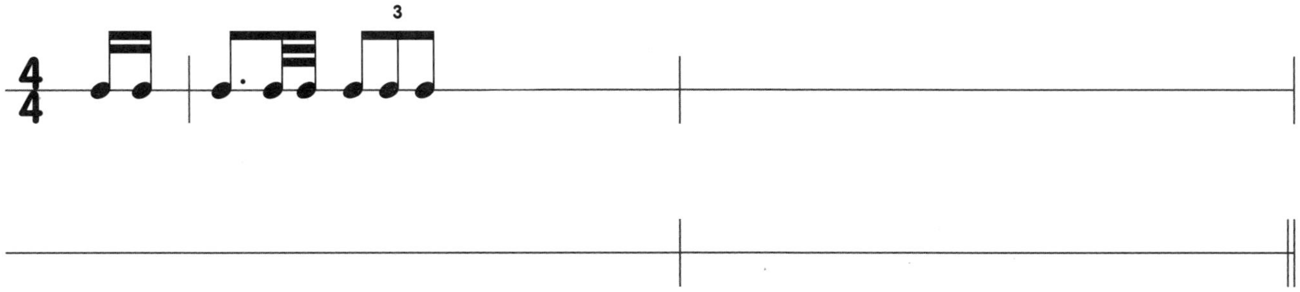

Double sharps and flats

- A **double sharp** (×) raises a note by 2 semitones.

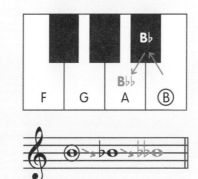

- A **double flat** (♭♭) lowers a note by 2 semitones.

Enharmonic equivalents

Enharmonic equivalents are notes that have the same pitch but different letter names.

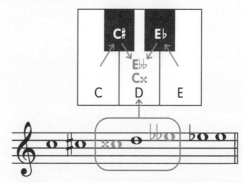

C× D E♭♭ are enharmonic equivalents.

1 Write the full name of each note. Then write as a semibreve (whole-note) **1 enharmonic equivalent.**

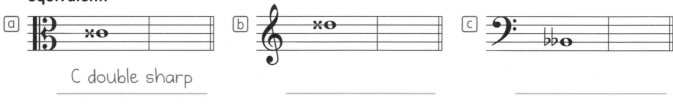

a) C double sharp

2 Name the enharmonic equivalents for each key.
(All the keys have 3 names, except G♯ and A♭, which has only 2 names.)

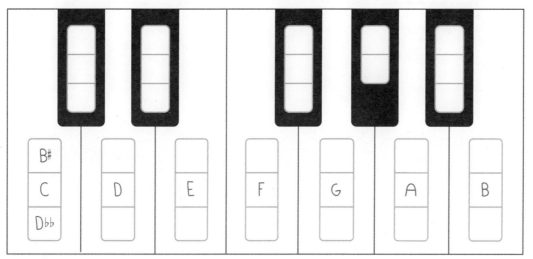

2 Finding the 2 enharmonic equivalents of a note:

• Find enharmonic equivalents by raising or lowering neighboring notes:

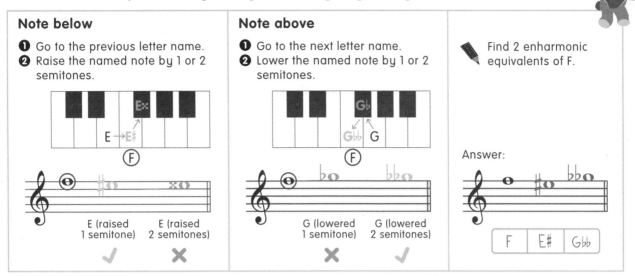

Note below
❶ Go to the previous letter name.
❷ Raise the named note by 1 or 2 semitones.

E (raised 1 semitone) ✓   E (raised 2 semitones) ✗

Note above
❶ Go to the next letter name.
❷ Lower the named note by 1 or 2 semitones.

G (lowered 1 semitone) ✗   G (lowered 2 semitones) ✓

Find 2 enharmonic equivalents of F.

Answer:

| F | E♯ | G♭♭ |

---

3 Write the letter name of each note. Then write as breves (double whole-notes) 2 enharmonic equivalents and their letter names.

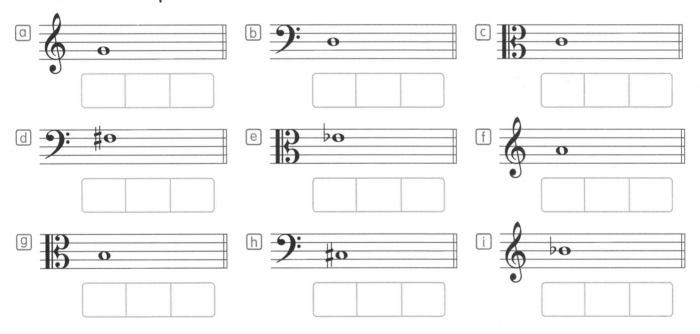

---

4 Add the accidental needed before each note marked ∗ to restore it to its original pitch. (Write a single sharp or flat to cancel only one of a pair of double sharps or flats.)

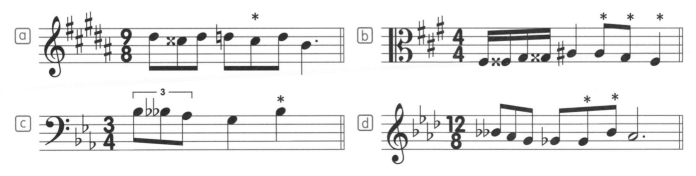

Scales with Five Sharps and Five Flats

1 **Write the letter names of the notes for the B major scale.**

B major

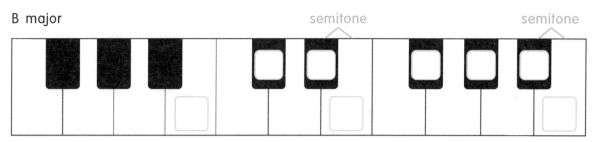

2 **Add the clef and any sharps or flats to make each scale named. Mark the semitones with ⌐.**

[a] B major, ascending

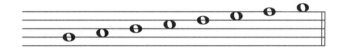

[b] B major, descending

3 **Copy each clef, key signature and key name.**

[a]

B major _____

[b]

B major _____

[c]

B major _____

4 **Write as semibreves** (whole-notes) **each scale named, with a key signature.**

[a] B major descending

[b] B major ascending

5 **Write as semibreves** (whole-notes) **each scale named, without a key signature but adding any sharps or flats.**

[a] B major descending

[b] B major ascending

6 Write the letter names of the notes for the D♭ major scale.

D♭ major

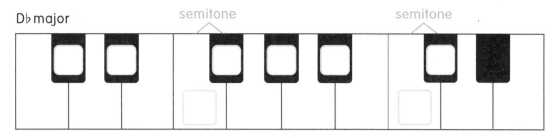

7 Add the clef and any sharps or flats to make each scale named. Mark the semitones with ⌐⌐.

a D♭ major, ascending

b D♭ major, descending

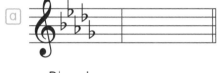

8 Copy each clef, key signature and key name.

a

D♭ major

b D♭ major

c D♭ major

9 Write as semibreves (whole-notes) each scale named, with a key signature.

a D♭ major
descending

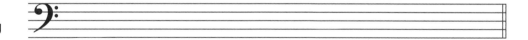

b D♭ major
ascending

10 Write as semibreves (whole-notes) each scale named, without a key signature but adding any sharps or flats.

a D♭ major
descending

b D♭ major
ascending

Relationship between major and minor keys

- The minor is 3 semitones down from its relative major; the major is 3 semitones up from its relative minor.

11 Fill in the keys and key signatures.

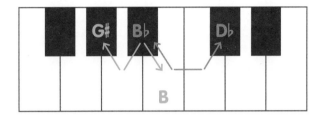

Major	Relative minor	Key signature
B major		F♯
D♭ major		B♭

Circle of 5ths

Grade 4 introduces major and minor scales with:
- 5 sharps: B major and G♯ minor. • 5 flats: D♭ major and B♭ minor.

 Building key signatures using the circle of 5ths: p. 32 in Music Theory for Young Musicians, Grade 3, 3rd Ed.

12 Fill in the keys in the circle of 5ths, and write the key signatures.

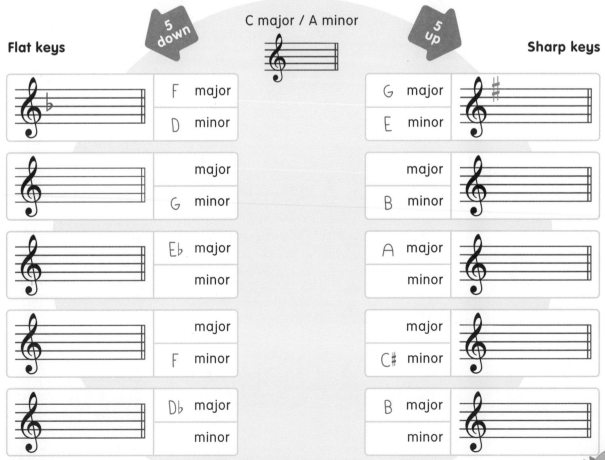

Minor scale: Harmonic minor

• Raise (or sharpen) the 7th note up and down.

With key signature	Without key signature

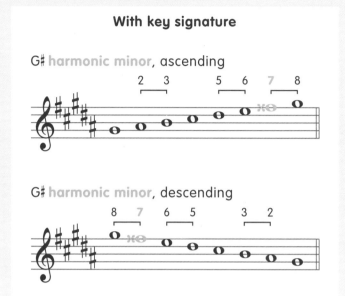

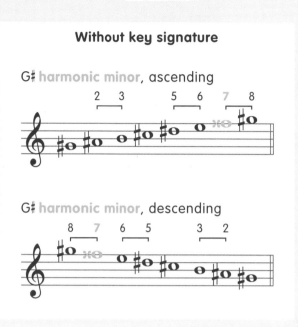

13 **Add the clef and key signature to make each** harmonic minor scale **named.** **(Raise the 7th note.)**

ⓐ G♯ harmonic minor

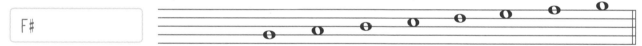

F♯

ⓑ B♭ harmonic minor

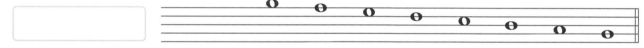

14 **Add the clef and any sharps or flats to make each** harmonic minor scale **named.** **(Do not use a key signature. Raise the 7th note.)**

ⓐ B♭ harmonic minor

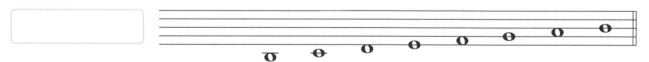

ⓑ G♯ harmonic minor

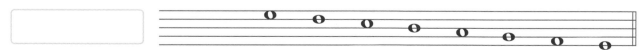

15 Write as semibreves (whole-notes) **each harmonic minor scale named, with a key signature. (Raise the 7th note.)**

a G# harmonic minor, descending

b B♭ harmonic minor, ascending

16 Write as semibreves (whole-notes) **each harmonic minor scale named, without a key signature but adding any sharps or flats. (Raise the 7th note.)**

a G# harmonic minor, ascending

b B♭ harmonic minor, descending

17 Write the key signature of 5 flats. Then write as semibreves (whole-notes) one octave ascending of the harmonic minor scale, with the key signature. (Begin on the tonic and add any sharps, flats or naturals.)

18 Write the key signature of 5 sharps. Then write as semibreves (whole-notes) one octave descending of the harmonic minor scale, with the key signature. (Begin on the tonic and add any sharps, flats or naturals.)

Minor scale: Melodic minor

• Raise (or sharpen) the 6th and 7th notes going up only.

With key signature	**Without key signature**
G♯ melodic minor, ascending 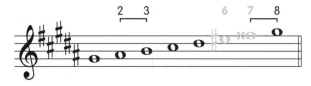	G♯ melodic minor, ascending 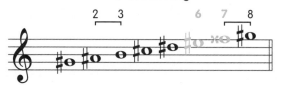
G♯ melodic minor, descending 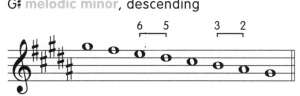	G♯ melodic minor, descending 

19 **Add the clef and key signature to make each** melodic minor scale **named. (Raise the 6th and 7th notes going up only.)**

ⓐ G♯ melodic minor

ⓑ B♭ melodic minor

20 **Add the clef and any sharps or flats to make each** melodic minor scale **named. (Do not use a key signature. Raise the 6th and 7th notes going up only.)**

ⓐ B♭ melodic minor

ⓑ G♯ melodic minor

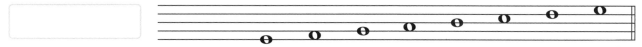

21 Write as semibreves (whole-notes) **each melodic minor scale named,** with a key signature. (Raise the 6th and 7th notes going up only.)

[a] G♯ melodic minor, descending

[b] B♭ melodic minor, ascending

22 Write as semibreves (whole-notes) **each melodic minor scale named,** without a key signature but adding any sharps or flats.
(Raise the 6th and 7th notes going up only.)

[a] B♭ melodic minor, descending

[b] G♯ melodic minor, ascending

23 Write the key signature of 5 sharps. Then write as semibreves (whole-notes) one octave descending of the melodic minor scale, with the key signature. (Begin on the tonic and add any sharps, flats or naturals.)

24 Write the key signature of 5 flats. Then write as semibreves (whole-notes) one octave ascending of the melodic minor scale, with the key signature. (Begin on the tonic and add any sharps, flats or naturals.)

25 **Add the clef and key signature to make each scale named.**
(Add any additional sharps, flats or naturals.)

a   B♭   harmonic
         minor

b   G♯   melodic
         minor
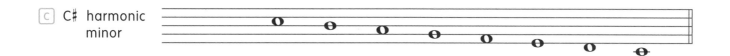

c   C♯   harmonic
         minor
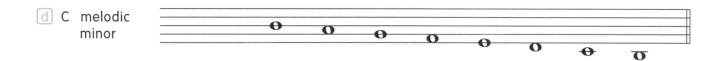

d   C   melodic
         minor

e   B   major

f   F   melodic
         minor
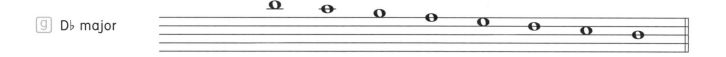

g   D♭   major

h   F♯   harmonic
         minor

i   A♭   major

Technical Names of Notes

Technical names

The technical names of the degrees of the scale, in ascending order, are:

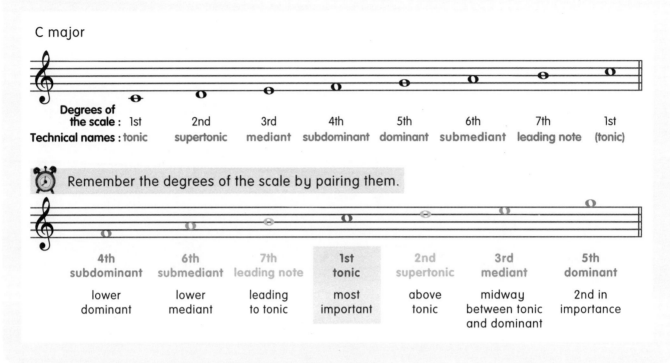

C major

Degrees of the scale :	1st	2nd	3rd	4th	5th	6th	7th	1st
Technical names :	tonic	supertonic	mediant	subdominant	dominant	submediant	leading note	(tonic)

⏰ Remember the degrees of the scale by pairing them.

4th subdominant	6th submediant	7th leading note	1st tonic	2nd supertonic	3rd mediant	5th dominant
lower dominant	lower mediant	leading to tonic	most important	above tonic	midway between tonic and dominant	2nd in importance

1 **Write the technical names of the degrees of the scale.**

1st	2nd	3rd	4th	5th	6th	7th

2 **Fill in the letter names for the degrees of the scale. Write the technical names of the numbered notes.**

a

G major	1st	2nd	3rd	4th	5th	6th	7th
Letter name	G	A					

1 _____   2 _____   3 _____

4 _____   5 _____   6 _____

D minor	1st	2nd	3rd	4th	5th	6th	7th
Letter name							

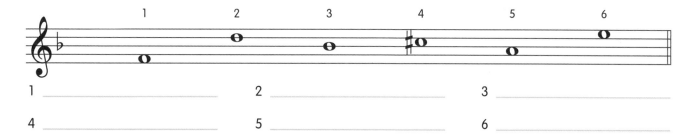

1 _____ 2 _____ 3 _____

4 _____ 5 _____ 6 _____

3 **Name the key of each of the following. Write the technical names of the numbered notes.**

(a)

Key _____ 1 _____ 2 _____ 3 _____

4 _____ 5 _____ 6 _____

(b)

Key _____ 1 _____ 2 _____ 3 _____

4 _____ 5 _____ 6 _____

(c)

Key _____ 1 _____ 2 _____ 3 _____

4 _____ 5 _____ 6 _____

(d)

Key _____ 1 _____ 2 _____ 3 _____

4 _____ 5 _____ 6 _____

Triads and Chords on I, IV and V

Triads and chords

- A **chord** is 3 or more notes played together.
- A **triad** is a 3-note chord that is built on 3rds.
- **Primary triads** are built on the 1st, 4th and 5th degrees of the scale, named as tonic (I), subdominant (IV) and dominant (V).

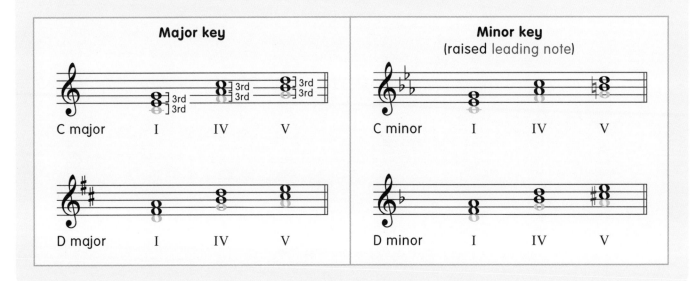

1 Write the key signature and primary triads (tonic, subdominant, dominant) for each key. Describe each triad as **I**, **IV** or **V**.

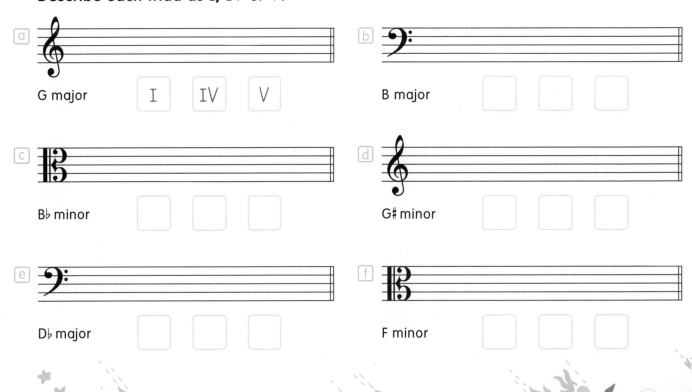

a G major   I   IV   V

b B major   ☐   ☐   ☐

c B♭ minor   ☐   ☐   ☐

d G♯ minor   ☐   ☐   ☐

e D♭ major   ☐   ☐   ☐

f F minor   ☐   ☐   ☐

2 Describe each triad as I, IV or V.

a. A major

b. E♭ major

c. C♯ minor

d. G minor

e. B major

f. B♭ minor

g. D♭ major

h. G♯ minor

3 Write the key signature and dominant triad for each minor key. (Raise the 7th note.)

a. B minor   V

b. F♯ minor   V

c. C♯ minor   V

d. G♯ minor   V

e. G minor   V

f. C minor   V

g. F minor   V

h. B♭ minor   V

4 Write each key signature and triad.

a. B♭ minor
    tonic

b. B major
    subdominant

c. E minor
    dominant

d. G♯ minor
    subdominant

e. C minor
    subdominant

f. A major
    tonic

g. D minor
    dominant

h. D♭ major
    subdominant

5 Write each triad given its key signature.

a)
major key
tonic

b)
minor key
subdominant

c)
minor key
dominant

d)
major key
subdominant

e)
minor key
tonic

f)
minor key
dominant

6 Add the clef and key signature to each triad.

a)
C minor
tonic

b)
Ab major
subdominant

c)
G# minor
dominant

7 Add the clef and any sharps or flats to each triad. (Do not use a key signature.)

a)
D major
tonic

b)
Bb minor
subdominant

c)
C# minor
dominant

8 Name the key of each triad, and describe it as tonic (I), subdominant (IV) or dominant (V).

a)
Key _____
Triad _____

b)
Key _____
Triad _____

c)
Key _____
Triad _____

d)
Key _____
Triad _____

e)
Key _____
Triad _____

f)
Key _____
Triad _____

2 Extending on the triads: Note doubling

- A 4-note chord is made up of a triad + a doubled 1st or 5th.

9 **Describe each numbered chord as tonic (I), subdominant (IV) or dominant (V).**

a The key is F major.

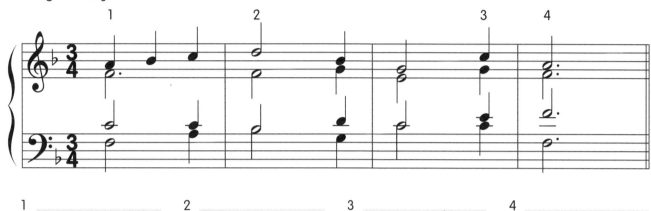

1 _____ 2 _____ 3 _____ 4 _____

b The key is A minor.

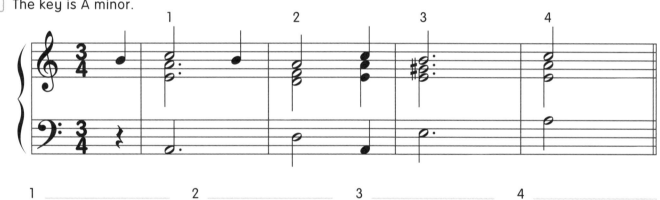

1 _____ 2 _____ 3 _____ 4 _____

c The key is F minor.

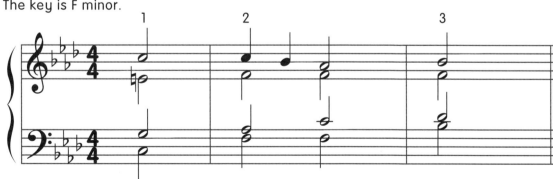

1 _____ 2 _____ 3 _____

Interval type

- The type of an interval is either major, minor, perfect, diminished or augmented.
- In a major key, an interval is either perfect (4th, 5th, or 8ve) or major (2nd, 3rd, 6th, or 7th).

Perfect, diminished and augmented intervals

- Unisons, octaves, 4ths, and 5ths are **perfect** intervals in a major key.
- A **diminished** interval is a semitone smaller than a perfect interval.
- An **augmented** interval is a semitone larger than a perfect interval.

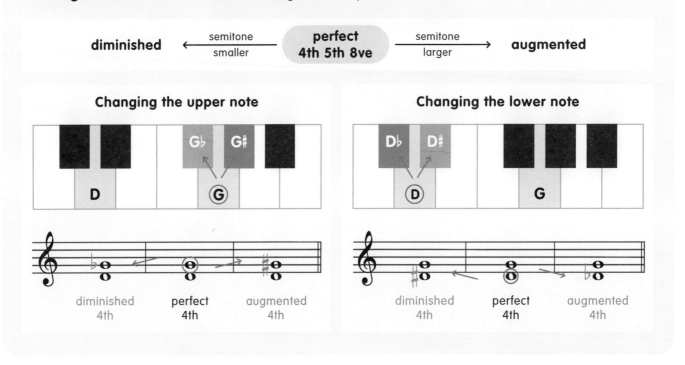

1 Add any sharps or flats to each upper note to make the correct interval type.

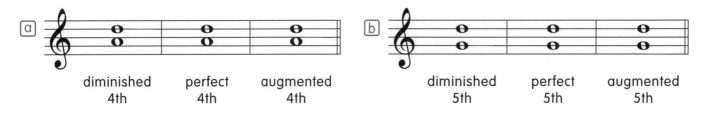

2 Add any sharps or flats to each lower note to make the correct interval type.

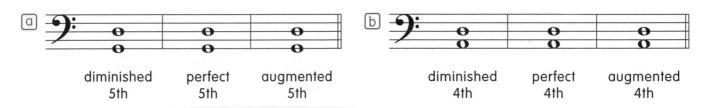

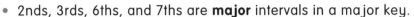

2 Major, minor, diminished and augmented intervals

- 2nds, 3rds, 6ths, and 7ths are **major** intervals in a major key.
- A **minor** interval is a semitone smaller than a major interval.
- A **diminished** interval is a semitone smaller than a minor interval.
- An **augmented** interval is a semitone larger than a major interval.

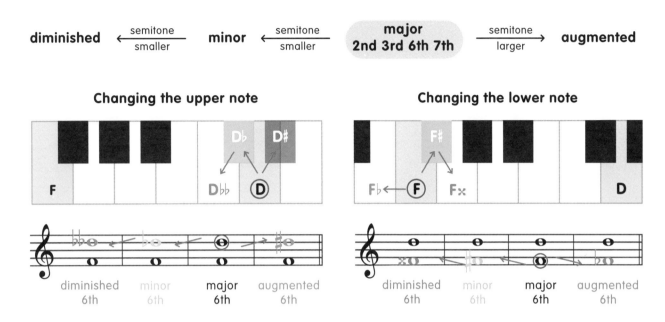

3 Add any sharps or flats to each upper note to make the correct interval type.

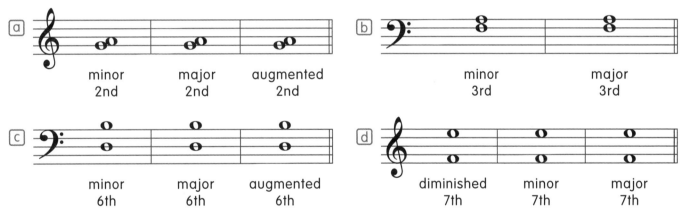

4 Add any sharps or flats to each lower note to make the correct interval type.

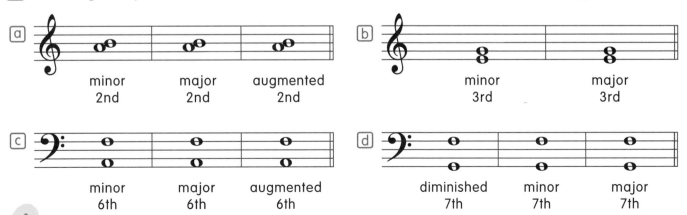

Finding the type of an interval: Dressing method

• Compare the interval to a major interval and determine how many semitones of difference exist:

❶ Remove accidentals. Then build a major scale on the lower note.
❷ Put on accidentals. Then compare each note to the major scale note.

Identify the number and type for each interval.

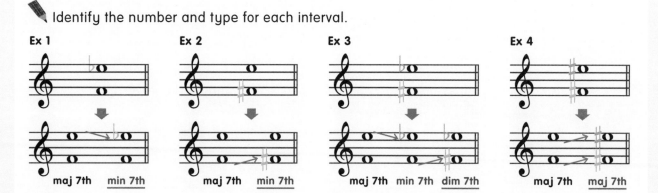

5 Identify the number and type for each interval (e.g. minor 2nd, perfect 5th).

40 | Intervals

6 **Identify the number and quality for each numbered** melodic interval **(e.g. minor 2nd, perfect 5th).**

1 _____ 2 _____ 3 _____

4 _____ 5 _____ 6 _____

1 _____ 2 _____ 3 _____

4 _____ 5 _____ 6 _____

7 **Identify the number and type for each numbered** harmonic interval **(e.g. minor 2nd, perfect 5th).**

1 _____ 2 _____ 3 _____

4 _____ 5 _____ 6 _____

1 _____ 2 _____ 3 _____

4 _____ 5 _____ 6 _____

Chromatic Scale

Chromatic scale

- A chromatic scale (chromatic means 'coloured') has 12 notes, and each step of the scale is a semitone. The scales are colourful as they use all 12 possible notes available instead of 7 of them.
- Use the keyboard as a visual aid.

Add accidentals to the following to make a chromatic scale.

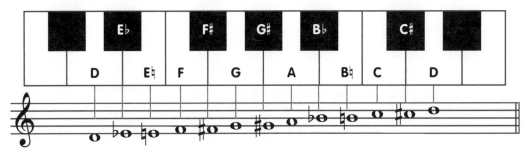

The 1st and last (13th) note is the tonic.

1 Add accidentals to each of the following to make a chromatic scale beginning on the given note.

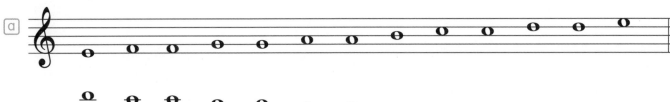

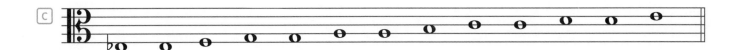

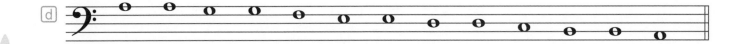

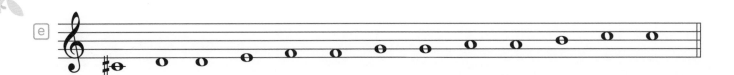

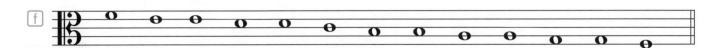

Adding accidentals: With a key signature

• Note the key signature and then put a mark above the notes that are sharped or flatted throughout the piece.

✎ Add accidentals to the following to make a chromatic scale.

2 **Add accidentals to each of the following to create a chromatic scale beginning on the given note. (Use the keyboard as a visual aid.)**

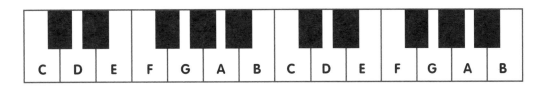

ⓐ

ⓑ

ⓒ

ⓓ

ⓔ

Writing a chromatic scale

Here are two methods to write a chromatic scale:

Method 1: Harmonic chromatic

❶ Use all notes twice (except for the tonic and dominant).
❷ Add sharps, flats and naturals to the notes.

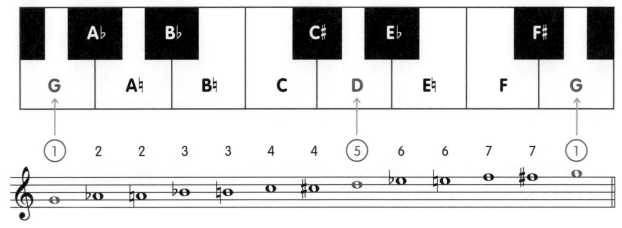

ascending, starting on G

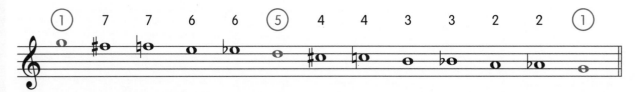

descending, starting on G

Method 2: Melodic chromatic

❶ Use at least 1 note, but not more than 2 for each line and space.
❷ Use sharps ascending and flats descending.

ascending, starting on C

descending, starting on C

3 **Write as semibreves** (whole-notes) **a chromatic scale beginning on each given note. (Do not use a key signature, but add any necessary sharps or flats.)**

a ascending, starting on G

b descending, starting on A♭

c ascending, starting on F♯

d descending, starting on E♭

e ascending, starting on D

4 **Draw ⌐ over 4 notes next to each other that form part of a chromatic scale.**

a

b

c

etc

Ornaments

Ornaments

- An **ornament** (or embellishment) decorates a melody by adding extra notes; it allows music to be more expressive.
- Baroque music is characterized by extensive use of ornamentation.

Symbol and name
- In grade 4, you need to be able to recognize and name the following ornaments:

Name	Symbol	Written	Played
acciaccatura (crushed note, grace note)			
acciaccature (crushed notes, grace notes)			
appoggiatura (leaning note)		ⓐ ⓑ	ⓐ ⓑ
upper turn (turn)		ⓐ ⓑ	ⓐ ⓑ
upper mordent		ⓐ ⓑ	ⓐ ⓑ
lower mordent		ⓐ ⓑ	ⓐ ⓑ
trill (shake)	*tr*	*tr*	

1 Write the name of each ornament.

a _____ b _____ c _____ d _____

e _____ f _____ g _____ h _____

2 Write the name of each numbered ornament.

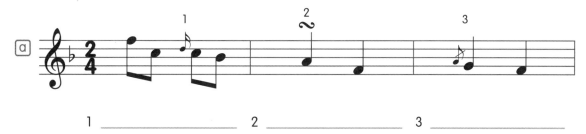

1 _____ 2 _____ 3 _____

1 _____ 2 _____ 3 _____

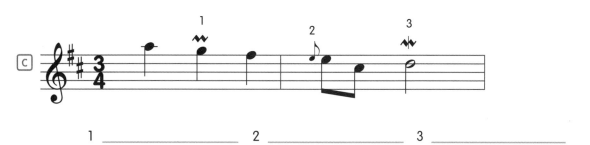

1 _____ 2 _____ 3 _____

3 Write each ornament symbol.

[a] upper mordent [ ]   [b] lower mordent [ ]   [c] appoggiatura [ ]   [d] turn [ ]

[e] appoggiatura [ ]   [f] acciaccatura [ ]   [g] acciaccature [ ]   [h] trill [ ]

4 Add the ornament symbol above each note marked ↑ .

[a] a trill

Chopin

[b] a turn

Mozart

[c] an upper mordent

WA Mozart

[d] a lower mordent

Handel

[e] an appoggiatura

Mozart

[f] an acciaccatura

Chopin

Writing an 8-bar rhythm to fit words

1. Underline every syllable.
2. Mark over each strong syllable.

>   >   >   >

Cob bler, cob bler, mend my shoe,

>   >   >   >

Get it done by half past two.   *Nursery Rhyme*

3. Draw a bar-line before each mark.
4. Choose a time signature. Then write a note value for each syllable.

Write a rhythm for the words.

Ex 1: Simple
- Set each syllable to a note.

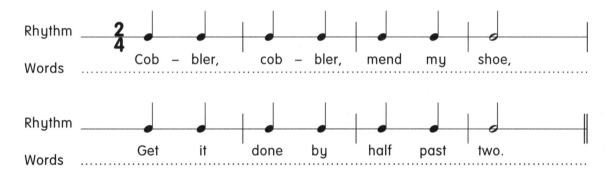

Ex 2: Improved
- Use notes of varying durations to create variety and interest.

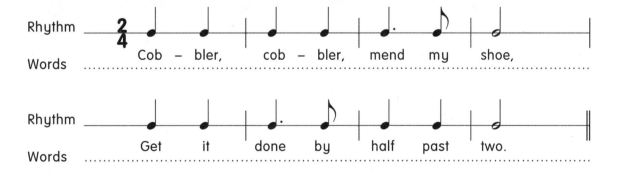

1 **Write a rhythm for the words.**

a   Tiger, tiger, burning bright

           In the forests of the night.   *William Blake*

Rhythm _____

Words ....

Rhythm _____

Words ....

b   How happy is the little stone

           That rambles in the road alone.   *Emily Dickinson*

Rhythm _____

Words ....

Rhythm _____

Words ....

c

Pussycat, pussycat, where have you been?

I've been to London to visit the Queen.   *Nursery Rhyme*

Rhythm _____

Words ....

Rhythm _____

Words ....

d

Peter, Peter, pumpkin eater,

Had a wife and couldn't keep her.   *Nursery Rhyme*

Rhythm _____

Words ....

Rhythm _____

Words ....

Instruments

Orchestral families

In a symphony orchestra, there are 4 families of instruments: **strings**, **woodwind**, **brass** and **percussion**.

String family
- String instruments have 4 strings.
- A string instrument is played by drawing a bow across the strings, or plucking or tapping the strings with the fingers.
- They can play **more than one note** at a time, and can play '**con sordini**' (with mutes).

highest-sounding ←————————→ lowest-sounding

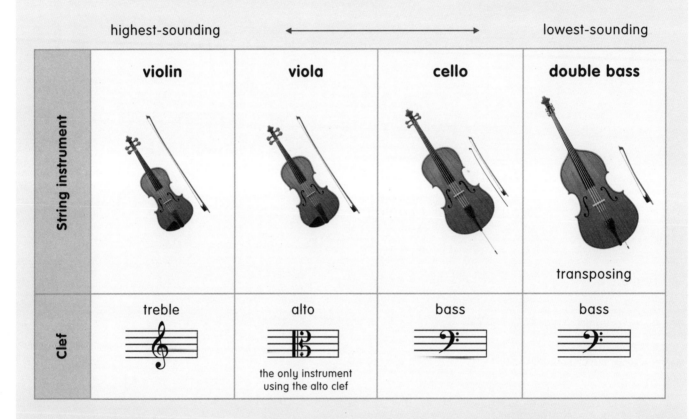

	violin	viola	cello	double bass
String instrument				transposing
Clef	treble	alto the only instrument using the alto clef	bass	bass

Performance directions

arco	: bowing	**sul G**	: play on the G string
pizzicato (pizz.)	: plucking	**sul ponticello**	: play near the bridge
con sordino (con sord.)	: with mute		: played in a single bow stroke (up or down)
con sordini	: with mutes		
senza sordino (senza sord.)	: without mute	⊓	: down bow
senza sordini	: without mutes		
		V	: up bow

1 **Complete the table by naming the string instruments and their clefs.**

Instrument	violin			
Clef	treble			

2 **Answer each of the following.**

a Name the highest-sounding string instrument. _____

b Name a string instrument that normally uses the alto clef. _____

c Name a string instrument that can play music written in the treble clef. _____

d Name 2 string instruments that can play music written in the bass clef.

_____ and _____

e A double bass player may be asked to play '**con sordini**'. _____ (TRUE/FALSE)

3 **Complete each of the following.**

a The violin belongs to the _____ family.

b The lowest-sounding string instrument is the _____ and it normally uses

the _____ clef.

c '**pizz. (pizzicato)**' means _____ and the family that

may be played in this way is the _____ family.

4 **Give the meaning of:**

a **arco** _____

b **con sordini** _____

c **sul G** _____

d **sul ponticello** _____

e **V** _____

f **senza sordini** _____

g **⌐** _____

h

2 Woodwind family

- Woodwind instruments are long narrow tubes with holes.
- A woodwind instrument is played by blowing across or into the tube.
- They can play **only one note** at a time.

highest-sounding ⟵⟶ lowest-sounding

Woodwind instrument	flute	oboe	clarinet	bassoon
			transposing	
Clef	treble	treble	treble	bass

5 Complete the table by naming the woodwind instruments and their clefs.

Instrument	flute			
Clef	treble			

6 Answer each of the following.

ⓐ Name the highest-sounding woodwind instrument. _____

ⓑ Name a woodwind instrument that
cannot play music written in the treble clef. _____

ⓒ Name 2 woodwind instruments that can play music written in the treble clef.

_____ and _____

7 Complete the following.

ⓐ The oboe belongs to the _____ family and the lowest-sounding

member of that family is the _____

3

Brass family
- Brass instruments are long tubes of curved brass.
- A brass instrument is played by blowing through a reed, or buzzing into a mouthpiece.
- They can play **only one note** at a time, and can play 'con sordini' (with mutes).

highest-sounding ←————————————————→ lowest-sounding

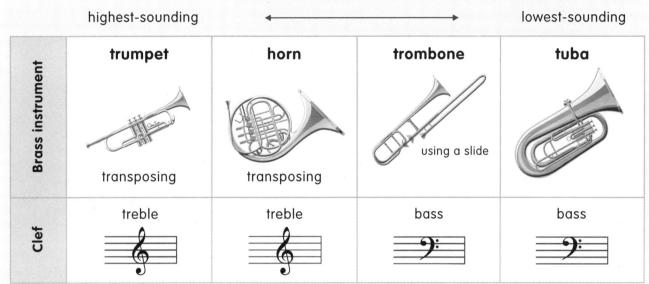

Brass instrument	trumpet	horn	trombone	tuba
	transposing	transposing	using a slide	
Clef	treble	treble	bass	bass

8 **Complete the table by naming the brass instruments and their clefs.**

Instrument	trumpet			
Clef	treble			

9 **Answer each of the following.**

a Name the highest-sounding brass instrument. _____

b No solo member of the brass or woodwind family can play more than one note at a time.

_____ (TRUE/FALSE)

c Underline 2 instruments, one string and one brass, that may be played 'con sordini'.

flute   trumpet   clarinet   violin

10 **Complete each of the following.**

a The lowest-sounding brass instrument is the _____ and it normally uses

the _____ clef.

b The _____ uses a slide to produce sound.

Percussion family
- Percussion instruments are classified as definite pitch or indefinite pitch.
- A percussion instrument is played by hitting, shaking or scraping it.

Definite pitch		Clef	Indefinite pitch
timpani (kettle drums) the only drums producing notes in definite pitch		bass 𝄢	**side drum**
glockenspiel		treble 𝄞	**bass drum**
			cymbals
xylophone		treble 𝄞	**triangle**

---

11 Answer each of the following.

a Name 2 percussion instruments that produce notes of indefinite pitch. (i) _____

(ii) _____

b The timpani are the only drums that can produce notes in definite pitch. _____ (TRUE/FALSE)

c Underline 2 instruments that are not members of the percussion family.

    timpani   tuba   cymbals   bassoon   bass drum

12 Complete each of the following.

a The bass drum belongs to the _____ family.

b The music for the timpani is written in the _____ clef.

c The timpani are sometimes called _____ .

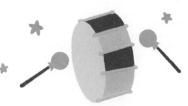

Piano

- Piano is a percussion instrument played by means of a keyboard; pressing a key on the keyboard causes a hammer to strike strings.

grand piano

treble

bass

Performance directions

mano	: hand (**mano sinistra, m.s.**: left hand; **mano destra, m.d.**: right hand)	**una corda (1 string)**	: press the left pedal
pedale	: pedal (**con pedale**: with pedal)	**tre corde (3 strings)**	: release the left pedal
	: spread the notes of the chord quickly, starting from the bottom	𝄚 ✼ or *p*_____	: press or release the right pedal

13 **Give the meaning of:**

a) **una corda** _____

b) **mano sinistra** _____

c) **tre corde** _____

d) **con pedale** _____

e) **mano destra** _____

f) *p*_____ _____

Performance Directions

Italian terms

a	at, to, by, for, in the style of
accelerando (accel.)	gradually getting quicker
ad libitum (ad lib.)	at choice, freely
Adagietto	rather slow (quicker than **Adagio**)
Adagio	slow
affettuoso	tenderly
affrettando	hurrying
agitato	agitated
al, alla	to the, in the manner of (**alla breve**: with a minim beat, ¢ (2/2); **alla marcia**: in the style of a march)
Allargando	broadening (getting slower and louder)
Allegretto	fairly quick (slower than **Allegro**)
Allegro	lively, quick (**Allegro assai**: very quick)
amabile	amiable, pleasant
amore	love (*amoroso*: loving)
Andante	at a walking/medium speed
Andantino	slightly quicker (or slower) than **Andante**
anima	soul, spirit (*con anima*: with spirit)
animando	becoming lively
animato	animated, lively
appassionato	with passion
assai	very
ben	well
brio	vigour (*con brio*: with vigour)
calando	getting quieter, dying away
cantabile	in a singing style
cantando	singing

come	as, similar to (*come prima*: as before; *come sopra*: as above)
comodo	convenient, comfortable (**tempo comodo**: at a comfortable (normal) speed)
con, col	with
crescendo (cresc.)	gradually getting louder
da capo (D.C.)	repeat from the beginning
dal segno (D.S.)	repeat from the sign 𝄋
deciso	with determination
decrescendo (decresc.)	gradually getting quieter
delicato	delicate
diminuendo (dim.)	gradually getting quieter
dolce	sweet
e, ed	and
energico	energetic
espressivo (express., espr.)	expressive (*espressione*: expression; *con espressione*: with expression)
***f* (forte)**	loud
facile	easy
***ff* (fortissimo)**	very loud
Fine	the end
forza	force
***fp* (fortepiano)**	loud, then immediately quiet
fuoco	fire
***fz* (forzando)**	forced, accented
giocoso	playful, merry
giusto	proper, exact (*tempo giusto*: in strict time)
grave	solemn, very slow
grazioso	graceful
l'istesso	the same (*l'istesso tempo*: at the same speed)

Newly introduced terms for grade 4 are highlighted in colour.

Italian terms (Cont.)

Largamente	broadly	*risoluto*	bold, strong
Larghetto	rather slow (quicker than **Largo**)	**ritardando** (ritard., rit.)	gradually getting slower
Largo	slow, stately	**ritenuto** (riten., rit.)	held back
legato	smoothly		
leggiero	light, nimble	*ritmico*	rhythmically
Lento	slow	*rubato,*	with some freedom of time
ma	but	*tempo rubato*	
maestoso	majestic	*scherzando,*	playful, joking
marcato (marc.)	emphatic, accented	*scherzoso*	
marziale	in a military style	*seconda, secondo*	second
meno	less	*semplice*	simple, plain
mesto	sad	*sempre*	always
mezzo	half	*senza*	without
mf (**mezzo forte**)	moderately loud	*sf, sfz* (**sforzando, sforzato**)	forced, accented
moderato	moderately (**Allegro moderato**: moderately quick)	*simile (sim.)*	in the same way
molto	very, much	*sonoro*	resonant, with rich tone
morendo	dying away	*sopra*	above
mosso, moto	movement (**meno mosso**: slower) (*con moto*: with movement)	*sostenuto*	sustained
		sotto	below (*sotto voce*: in an undertone)
mp (**mezzo piano**)	moderately quiet	*staccato (stacc.)*	detached
niente	nothing (*a niente*: dying away)	**stringendo**	gradually getting quicker
		subito	suddenly
nobilmente	nobly	*tanto*	so much
non	not	**tempo**	speed, time (**a tempo** : in time)
p (**piano**)	quiet		
perdendosi	dying away	*tenuto*	held
pesante	heavy	*tranquillo*	calm
più	more (**più mosso**: more movement)	*triste, tristamente*	sad, sorrowful
poco	a little	*troppo*	too much (**non troppo**: not too much)
possibile	possible (*presto possibile*: as fast as possible)	*veloce*	swift
pp (**pianissimo**)	very quiet	**vivace, vivo**	lively, quick
presto	quick (quicker than **Allegro**)	*voce*	voice
prima, primo	first	*volta*	time (*prima volta*: 1st time; *seconda volta*: 2nd time)
quasi	as if, resembling		
rallentando (rall.)	gradually getting slower		

French terms

à	to, at	*modéré*	at a moderate speed
animé	animated, lively	*non*	not
assez	enough, sufficiently	*peu*	little
avec	with	*plus*	more
cédez	yield, slow	*presser*	hurry (*en pressant*: hurrying on)
douce	sweet	*ralentir*	slow down
en dehors	prominent	*retenu*	held back (*en retenant*:
et	and		holding back, slowing a little)
expressif	expressive	*sans*	without
légèrement	light	*très*	very
lent	slow	*un, une*	one
mais	but	*vif*	lively
moins	less	*vite*	fast

Musical signs

pause: pause on the note or rest	(crescendo)	gradually getting louder
accent: accent the note	(diminuendo)	gradually getting quieter
marcato: play strongly accented	8va	octave
staccato: play detached		
semi-staccato: play slightly separated	8va 8	perform an octave higher
super-staccato (staccatissimo): play as short as possible	8va 8	perform an octave lower
tenuto: play with slight pressure		
dot: increase by half note value	**repeat marks**: repeat everything between repeat marks	
tie: perform the 1st note and hold for the value of both notes	and	
slur: perform the notes smoothly	♩ = 96	96 crotchet beats in a minute

1 **Underline one word from the list that has a similar meaning to each given word.**

a) *dolce* : *presser* *douce* *animé*

b) **Allegro** : *lent* *vite* *ralentir*

c) *leggiero* : *modéré* *légèrement* *lent*

d) **ritenuto** : *très* *ralentir* *retenu*

e) **Largo** : *lent* *peu* *légèrement*

f) **Vivace** : *douce* *vif* *cédez*

g) **più** : *peu* *plus* *presser*

h) **meno** : *moins* *sans* *mais*

i) *con* : *avec* *non* *très*

j) *senza* : *vite* *assez* *sans*

2 **Give the meaning of:**

a) *poco rit.* _____

b) *tranquillo* _____

c) **Allegro non troppo** _____

d) **affettuoso** _____

e) **più lento** _____

f) *quasi triste* _____

g) **Vivace ma non troppo** _____

h) **andante grazioso** _____

i) *poco a poco cresc.* _____

j) **molto vivace** _____

k) *largo sostenuto* _____

l) *un poco adagio* _____

m) *sotto voce* _____

n) **andante con moto** _____

o) *cantabile con espressione* _____

2 **Tick the correct box for each term/sign.**

Italian Terms

a) *affettuoso* means:
- [ ] at choice, freely
- [ ] quick
- [ ] tenderly
- [ ] hurrying

b) *amabile* means:
- [ ] amiable, pleasant
- [ ] at choice, freely
- [ ] love
- [ ] soul, spirit

c) *appassionato* means:
- [ ] broadening
- [ ] quick
- [ ] becoming lively
- [ ] with passion

d) *cantando* means:
- [ ] tenderly
- [ ] singing
- [ ] calm
- [ ] dying away

e) **con anima** means:
- [ ] with a minim beat
- [ ] with love
- [ ] with spirit
- [ ] with some freedom of time

f) *come prima* means:
- [ ] dying away
- [ ] as above
- [ ] singing
- [ ] as before

g) *l'istesso* means:
- [ ] calm
- [ ] dying away
- [ ] at the same speed
- [ ] the same

h) *morendo* means:
- [ ] becoming more lively
- [ ] calm
- [ ] dying away
- [ ] nothing

i) *perdendosi* means:
- [ ] tenderly
- [ ] heavy
- [ ] dying away
- [ ] with passion

j) *quasi* means:
- [ ] calm
- [ ] held
- [ ] as if, resembling
- [ ] more

k) **Scherzando** means:
- [ ] sad, sorrowful
- [ ] playful, joking
- [ ] simple, plain
- [ ] delicate

l) **senza rall.** means:
- [ ] held back
- [ ] getting faster
- [ ] without getting slower
- [ ] slow

m *sonoro* means:
- [ ] in an undertone
- [ ] resonant, with rich tone
- [ ] with passion
- [ ] sustained

n *sotto voce* means:
- [ ] in an undertone
- [ ] resonant, with rich tone
- [ ] below
- [ ] simple, plain

o **stringendo** means:
- [ ] gradually getting faster
- [ ] gradually getting slower
- [ ] in a singing style
- [ ] gradually getting quieter

p *sfz* means:
- [ ] slight pressure
- [ ] forced, accented
- [ ] loud, then immediately quiet
- [ ] moderately loud

q **Tempo comodo** means:
- [ ] slow, stately
- [ ] first time
- [ ] at a comfortable speed
- [ ] in time

r **Tempo guisto** means:
- [ ] at the same speed
- [ ] with some freedom of time
- [ ] at a comfortable speed
- [ ] in strict time

s *tristamente* means:
- [ ] slow, stately
- [ ] heavy
- [ ] sad, sorrowful
- [ ] calm

t *veloce* means:
- [ ] swift
- [ ] too much
- [ ] first time
- [ ] in time

French Terms

a *assez* means:
- [ ] hurrying
- [ ] enough, sufficiently
- [ ] more
- [ ] proper, exact

b *cédez* means:
- [ ] more
- [ ] yield, slow
- [ ] but
- [ ] with

c *en dehors* means:
- [ ] prominent
- [ ] enough, sufficiently
- [ ] yield, slow
- [ ] less

d *légèrement* means:
- [ ] light
- [ ] at a moderate speed
- [ ] more
- [ ] less

e. *moins* means:

☐ more
☐ less
☐ prominent
☐ very

f. *ralentir* means:

☐ to, at
☐ slow down
☐ held back
☐ lively

g. *sans* means:

☐ slow down
☐ light
☐ without
☐ very

h. *un, une* means:

☐ not
☐ one
☐ without
☐ more

Musical Signs

a. means:

☐ accent the note
☐ legato: smoothly
☐ *staccato*: detached
☐ *staccato*: smoothly

b. means:

☐ pause on the note or rest
☐ accent the note
☐ perform an octave higher
☐ *staccato*: detached

c. means:

☐ slur: perform the notes smoothly
☐ tie: detached
☐ slur: detached
☐ tie: perform the 1st note and hold for the value of both notes

d. ♩ = 100 means:

☐ 100 crotchets (quarter-notes) in the melody
☐ 100 crotchets (quarter-notes) in a bar
☐ 100 crotchet (quarter-note) beats
☐ 100 crotchet (quarter-note) beats in a minute

e. means:

☐ slight pressure
☐ strong accent
☐ *staccato*
☐ *sforzando*

f. means:

☐ held back
☐ repeat mark
☐ the end
☐ double bar-line

g. *8va* ⌐ means:

☐ perform an octave lower
☐ pause on the note or rest
☐ perform an octave higher
☐ perform the notes smoothly

h. **6/4** time signature means:

☐ 3 minim (half-note) beats in a bar
☐ 2 dotted minim (dotted half-note) beats in a bar
☐ 6 crotchet (quarter-note) beats in a bar
☐ 2 dotted crotchet (dotted quarter-note) beats in a bar

General Exercises

1 **Look at the melody and answer each of the following.**

Lento   Chopin

a) Tick the correct meaning of **Lento**.

☐ slow   ☐ rather slow   ☐ broadly   ☐ but

b) Add the time signature at the beginning.

c) Add the correct rest(s) at ✳ to complete bar 1.

d) The key is G minor. Name a key that has the same key signature. _____

e) Give the bar that contains all 3 notes of the tonic triad. _____

f) The triplet in bar 2 means 3 quavers in the time of _____

g) Give the technical name (e.g. tonic, supertonic) of the 1st note of bar 2. _____

h) Write as a breve (double whole-note) an enharmonic equivalent of the last note of bar 2.

i) Identify (e.g. minor 2nd, perfect 5th) the harmonic interval marked ✳ in bar 3. _____

j) Give the name of the ornament in bar 4. _____

k) Draw ⌐ over 4 notes next to each other that form part of a chromatic scale.

l) Rewrite bar 1 in compound time without changing the rhythmic effect.
(Add the new time signature.)

m) Rewrite bar 4 using the alto clef, so that it sounds the same.
(Add the clef and key signature.)

2 **Look at the melody and answer each of the following.**

a) Tick the correct meaning of **Presto**.

☐ slow   ☐ heavy   ☐ quick   ☐ more

b) Describe the time signature as: simple or compound _____

duple, triple or quadruple _____

c) Give the time name (e.g. crotchet or quarter-note) of the shortest note. _____

d) Give the letter name of the lowest note. _____

e) Give the number of times this rhythm ♩♫ appears. _____

f) Give the name of the ornament in bar 6. _____

g) Name 2 major keys, one that contains all the notes in **X**   **X** _____
and another that contains all the notes in **Y**.
     Y _____

h) Write as a breve (double whole-note) an enharmonic equivalent of the 1st note of bar 2.

i) Rewrite bar 5 using notes of **twice the value**. (Add the new time signature.)

j) Name a string instrument that can play bar 4. _____

k) Name one similarity and one difference between bars 1 and 2.

Similarity _____

Difference _____

3 **Look at the melody and answer each of the following.**

[a] Describe the time signature as: simple or compound _____

duple, triple or quadruple _____

[b] Give the form of the minor scale used in bar 2. _____ (harmonic/melodic)

[c] Circle 3 notes next to each other that form the tonic triad of C minor.

[d] Give the number of demisemiquavers (32nd notes) the 1st note of bar 3 is worth. _____

[e] Identify (e.g. minor 2nd, perfect 5th) the melodic interval marked ⌐¬ in bar 2. _____

[f] Write as a breve (double whole-note) an enharmonic equivalent of the 1st note of bar 4.

[g] Rewrite bar 1 in simple time but without changing the rhythmic effect. (Add the new time signature.)

[h] Rewrite bar 5 using notes of half the value. (Add the new time signature.)

Specimen Test Grade 4

Duration: 2 hours

TOTAL MARKS
100

1 Look at the melody and answer each of the following.

15

Modéré

douce et expressif

[a] Tick the correct meaning of *douce et expressif*. [2]

☐ sweet and expressive

☐ slow but lively

☐ animated and lively

☐ more expressive

[b] Rewrite bar 1 in compound time without changing the rhythmic effect.
(Add the new time signature.)

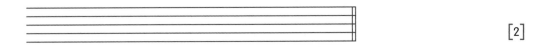

[2]

[c] Write as a breve (double whole-note) an enharmonic equivalent of the last note of bar 3.

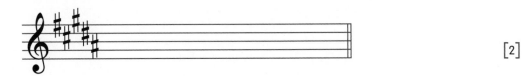

[2]

[d] Give the name of the ornament in bar 3. _____ [2]

[e] The key is B major. Name a key that has the same key signature.

_____ [2]

[f] Circle 3 notes next to each other that form the dominant triad of B major. [2]

[g] Give the technical name (e.g. tonic, supertonic) of the last note of bar 1.

_____

[2]

[h] Give the number of demisemiquavers (32nd notes) the last note of the melody

is worth. _____

[1]

2 [a] Describe each melodic interval (e.g. minor 2nd, perfect 5th).

[10]

_____

[b] After each note write a **higher** note to form the named **melodic** interval.

minor 7th   major 3rd

3 [a] Add accidentals to the following to make a chromatic scale beginning
on the given note.

[10]

[b] Write the key signature of 5 sharps. Then write as semibreves (whole-notes) one
octave ascending of the melodic minor scale, with the key signature.
(Begin on the tonic and add any sharps, flats or naturals.)

4 Look at the melody and answer each of the following.

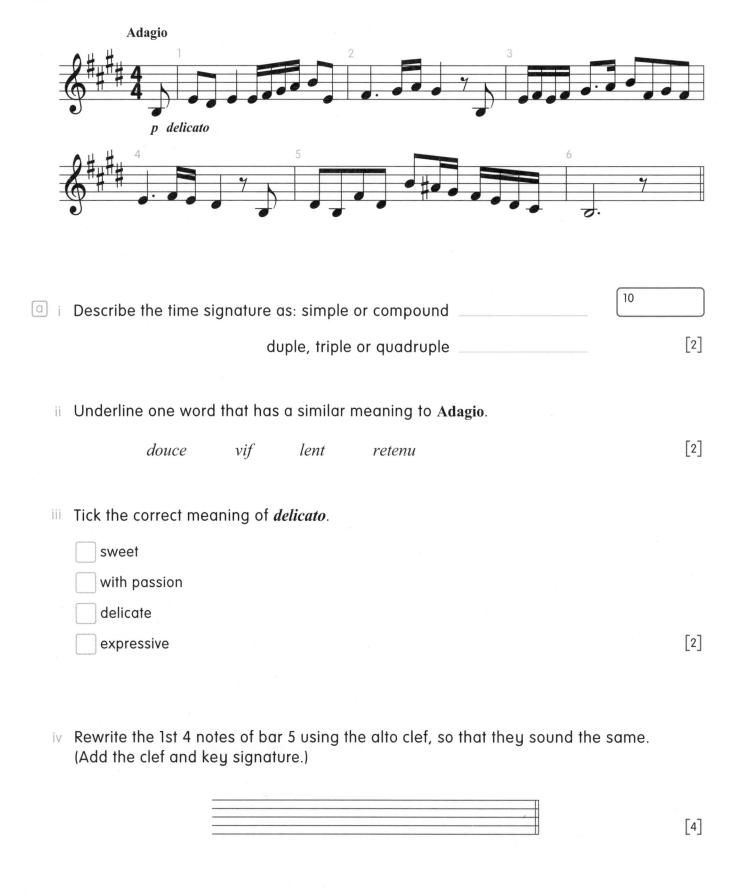

[a] i Describe the time signature as: simple or compound _____

duple, triple or quadruple _____ [2]

10

ii Underline one word that has a similar meaning to **Adagio**.

douce   *vif*   *lent*   *retenu* [2]

iii Tick the correct meaning of *delicato*.

☐ sweet

☐ with passion

☐ delicate

☐ expressive [2]

iv Rewrite the 1st 4 notes of bar 5 using the alto clef, so that they sound the same.
(Add the clef and key signature.)

[4]

b i The key is E major. Name a key that has the same key signature.

_____   [2]

ii Give the technical name (e.g. tonic, supertonic) of the 1st note of the melody.

_____   [2]

iii The melody starts in E major, but changes key from bar 5 onwards. Name the

key in which the notes of bars 5-6 can be found. _____   [2]

iv Rewrite bar 2 using notes and rests of half the value.
(Add the new time signature.)

[2]

v There are 2 melodic intervals of a perfect 5th in the melody. _____   [2]
(TRUE/FALSE)

c i Name an orchestral instrument that normally uses the treble clef,
and state the family to which it belongs.

Instrument _____   Family _____   [4]

ii Name the highest-sounding member of a different family
of orchestral instruments from the family you stated above. _____   [2]

iii Underline 2 percussion instruments that produce notes of definite pitch.

cymbals   timpani   side drum   xylophone   [4]

5 **a** Rewrite the treble notes at the same pitch in the alto clef.

b Rewrite the alto notes at the same pitch in the bass clef.

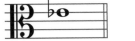  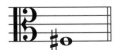 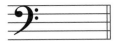

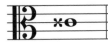 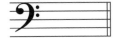

6 Rewrite each melody with the notes correctly grouped (or beamed).

etc.

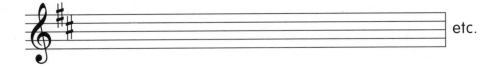

etc.

7 [a] Describe each numbered chord as tonic (I), subdominant (IV) or dominant (V). The key is F major.

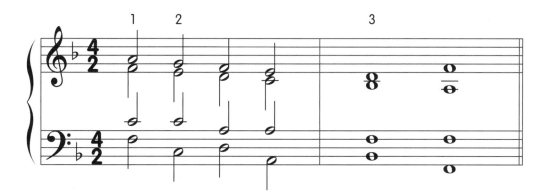

Chord: 1. _____   2. _____

3. _____   [9]

[b] Name the key of each triad, and describe it as tonic (I), subdominant (IV) or dominant (V).

Key _____   Key _____   Key _____

Triad _____   Triad _____   Triad _____

[6]

Revision Notes

Alto clef

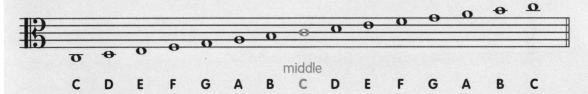

C D E F G A B middle C D E F G A B C

Notes and rests

Time name	breve (double whole-note)	semibreve (whole-note)	minim (half-note)	crotchet (quarter-note)	quaver (eighth-note)	semiquaver (16th note)	demisemiquaver (32nd note)
Note	𝄡	𝅝	𝅗𝅥	♩	♪	𝅘𝅥𝅯	𝅘𝅥𝅰
Rest	𝄻	𝄻	𝄼	𝄽	𝄾	𝄿	𝅀

- breve rest (double whole-note rest) = a whole bar rest in $\frac{4}{2}$
- semibreve rest (whole-note rest) = a whole bar rest in any time signature (except $\frac{4}{2}$)

Simple and compound time

	Simple time			Compound time		
Duple	$\frac{2}{2}$ 2 minim beats (half-note)	$\frac{2}{4}$ 2 crotchet beats (quarter-note)		$\frac{6}{4}$ 2 dotted minim beats (dotted half-note)	$\frac{6}{8}$ 2 dotted crotchet beats (dotted quarter-note)	$\frac{6}{16}$ 2 dotted quaver beats (dotted eighth-note)
Triple	$\frac{3}{2}$ 3 minim beats (half-note)	$\frac{3}{4}$ 3 crotchet beats (quarter-note)	$\frac{3}{8}$ 3 quaver beats (eighth-note)	$\frac{9}{4}$ 3 dotted minim beats (dotted half-note)	$\frac{9}{8}$ 3 dotted crotchet beats (dotted quarter-note)	$\frac{9}{16}$ 3 dotted quaver beats (dotted eighth-note)
Quadruple	$\frac{4}{2}$ 4 minim beats (half-note)	$\frac{4}{4}$ 4 crotchet beats (quarter-note)	$\frac{4}{8}$ 4 quaver beats (eighth-note)	$\frac{12}{4}$ 4 dotted minim beats (dotted half-note)	$\frac{12}{8}$ 4 dotted crotchet beats (dotted quarter-note)	$\frac{12}{16}$ 4 dotted quaver beats (dotted eighth-note)

Changing the time signature: Twice or half the value of the original

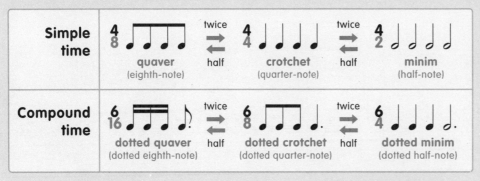

Simple time	$\frac{4}{8}$ quaver (eighth-note)	twice ⇄ half	$\frac{4}{4}$ crotchet (quarter-note)	twice ⇄ half	$\frac{4}{2}$ minim (half-note)
Compound time	$\frac{6}{16}$ dotted quaver (dotted eighth-note)	twice ⇄ half	$\frac{6}{8}$ dotted crotchet (dotted quarter-note)	twice ⇄ half	$\frac{6}{4}$ dotted minim (dotted half-note)

Changing the time signature: Simple and compound

Simple	$\frac{2}{2}$	$\frac{3}{2}$	$\frac{4}{2}$	$\frac{2}{4}$	$\frac{3}{4}$	$\frac{4}{4}$	$\frac{3}{8}$	$\frac{4}{8}$
Compound	$\frac{6}{4}$	$\frac{9}{4}$	$\frac{12}{4}$	$\frac{6}{8}$	$\frac{9}{8}$	$\frac{12}{8}$	$\frac{9}{16}$	$\frac{12}{16}$

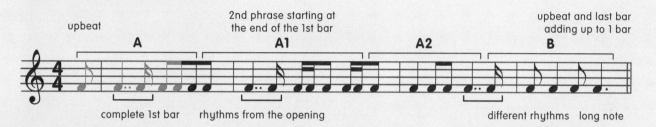

Composing a 4-bar rhythm

upbeat   **A**   2nd phrase starting at the end of the 1st bar   **A1**   **A2**   upbeat and last bar adding up to 1 bar   **B**

complete 1st bar   rhythms from the opening   different rhythms   long note

Key signatures

- Harmonic minor scale has a raised 7th scale degree up and down.
- Melodic minor scale has a raised 6th and 7th scale degrees going up only.

C major	G major	D major	A major	E major	B major
A minor	E minor	B minor	F♯ minor	C♯ minor	G♯ minor

F major	B♭ major	E♭ major	A♭ major	D♭ major
D minor	G minor	C minor	F minor	B♭ minor

Technical names of notes

1st	2nd	3rd	4th	5th	6th	7th	1st
tonic	supertonic	mediant	subdominant	dominant	submediant	leading note	(tonic)

Triads and Chords on I, IV and V

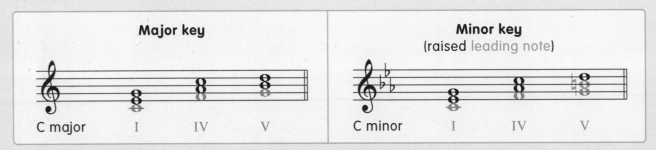

Intervals

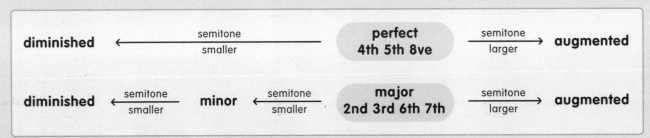

Ornaments

acciaccatura	acciaccature	appoggiatura	upper turn	upper mordent	lower mordent	trill / shake
♪	♫	♪	∼	∿	∿	tr

Instruments

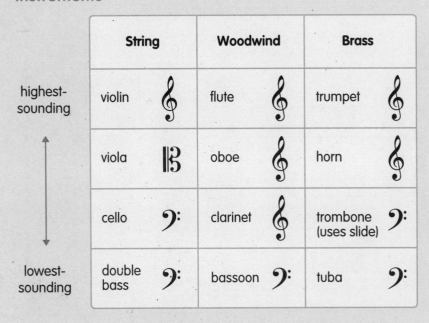

	String		Woodwind		Brass	
highest-sounding	violin	𝄞	flute	𝄞	trumpet	𝄞
	viola	𝄡	oboe	𝄞	horn	𝄞
	cello	𝄢	clarinet	𝄞	trombone (uses slide)	𝄢
lowest-sounding	double bass	𝄢	bassoon	𝄢	tuba	𝄢

Percussion	
Definite pitch	**Indefinte pitch**
timpani 𝄢	side drum
glockenspiel 𝄞	bass drum
	cymbals
xylophone 𝄞	triangle